WITHDRAWN

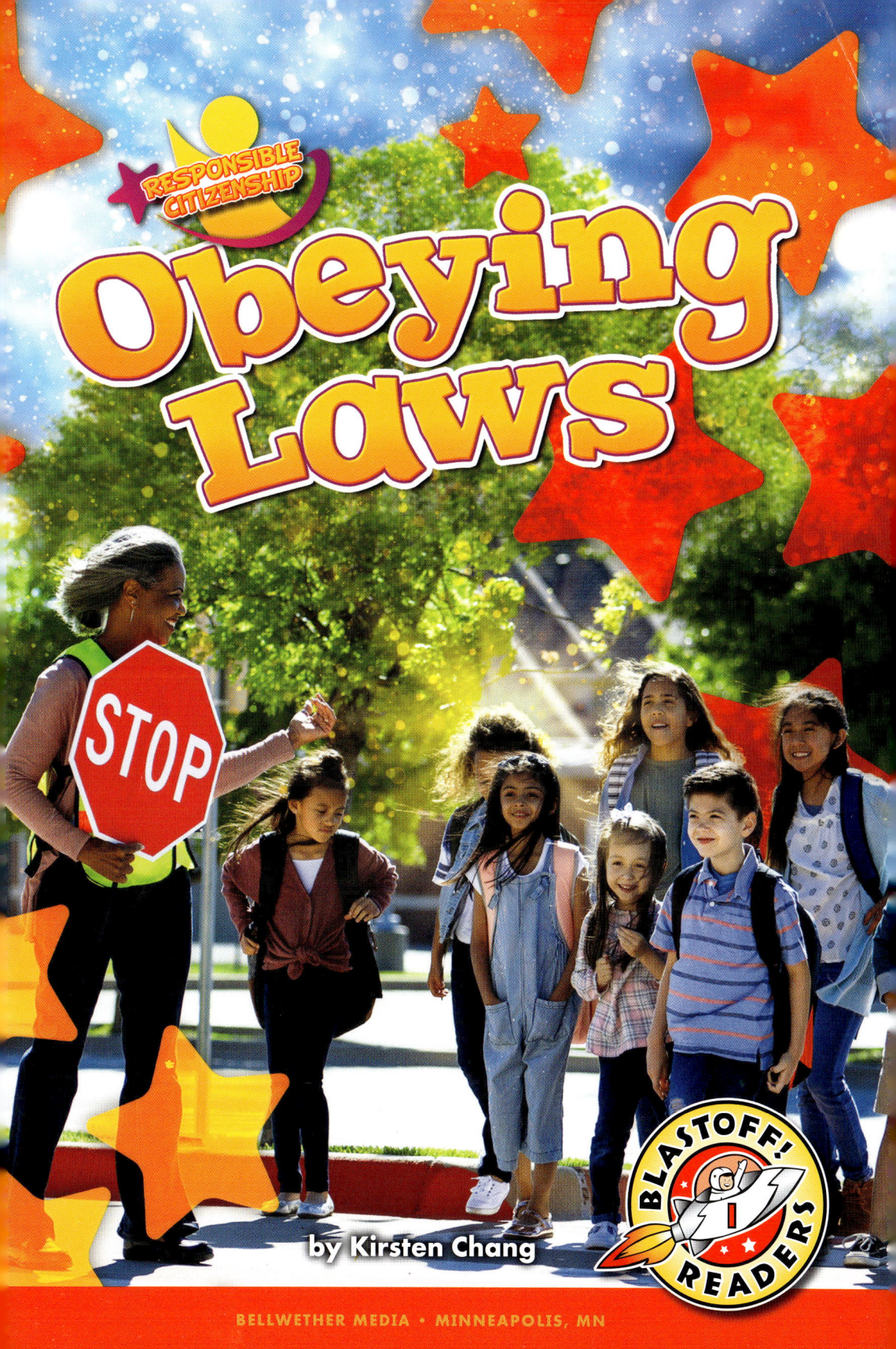

 **Blastoff! Readers** are carefully developed by literacy experts to build reading stamina and move students toward fluency by combining standards-based content with developmentally appropriate text.

 **Level 1** provides the most support through repetition of high-frequency words, light text, predictable sentence patterns, and strong visual support.

 **Level 2** offers early readers a bit more challenge through varied sentences, increased text load, and text-supportive special features.

 **Level 3** advances early-fluent readers toward fluency through increased text load, less reliance on photos, advancing concepts, longer sentences, and more complex special features.

★ **Blastoff! Universe**

Reading Level

  Grade K →   Grades 1–3 →   Grade 4

This edition first published in 2022 by Bellwether Media, Inc.

No part of this publication may be reproduced in whole or in part without written permission of the publisher. For information regarding permission, write to Bellwether Media, Inc., Attention: Permissions Department, 6012 Blue Circle Drive, Minnetonka, MN 55343.

Library of Congress Cataloging-in-Publication Data

Names: Chang, Kirsten, 1991- author.
Title: Obeying laws / by Kirsten Chang.
Description: Minneapolis, MN : Bellwether Media, Inc., 2022. | Series: Blastoff! Readers : responsible citizenship | Includes bibliographical references and index. | Audience: Ages 5-8 | Audience: Grades K-1 | Summary: "Developed by literacy experts for students in kindergarten through grade three, this book introduces obeying laws to young readers through leveled text and related photos" Provided by publisher.
Identifiers: LCCN (print) | LCCN 2021016565 (ebook) | ISBN 9781644874998 (library binding) | ISBN 9781648344756 (paperback) | ISBN 9781648344077 (ebook)
Subjects: LCSH: Rule of law–United States–Juvenile literature.
Classification: LCC KF382 .C43 2022 (print) | LCC KF382 (ebook) | DDC 340/.11–dc23
LC record available at https://lccn.loc.gov/2021016565
LC ebook record available at https://lccn.loc.gov/2021016565

Text copyright © 2022 by Bellwether Media, Inc. BLASTOFF! READERS and associated logos are trademarks and/or registered trademarks of Bellwether Media, Inc.

Editor: Kieran Downs   Designer: Brittany McIntosh

Printed in the United States of America, North Mankato, MN.

Table of Contents

Following the Rules	4
What Are Laws?	6
Why Is Obeying Laws Important?	16
Glossary	22
To Learn More	23
Index	24

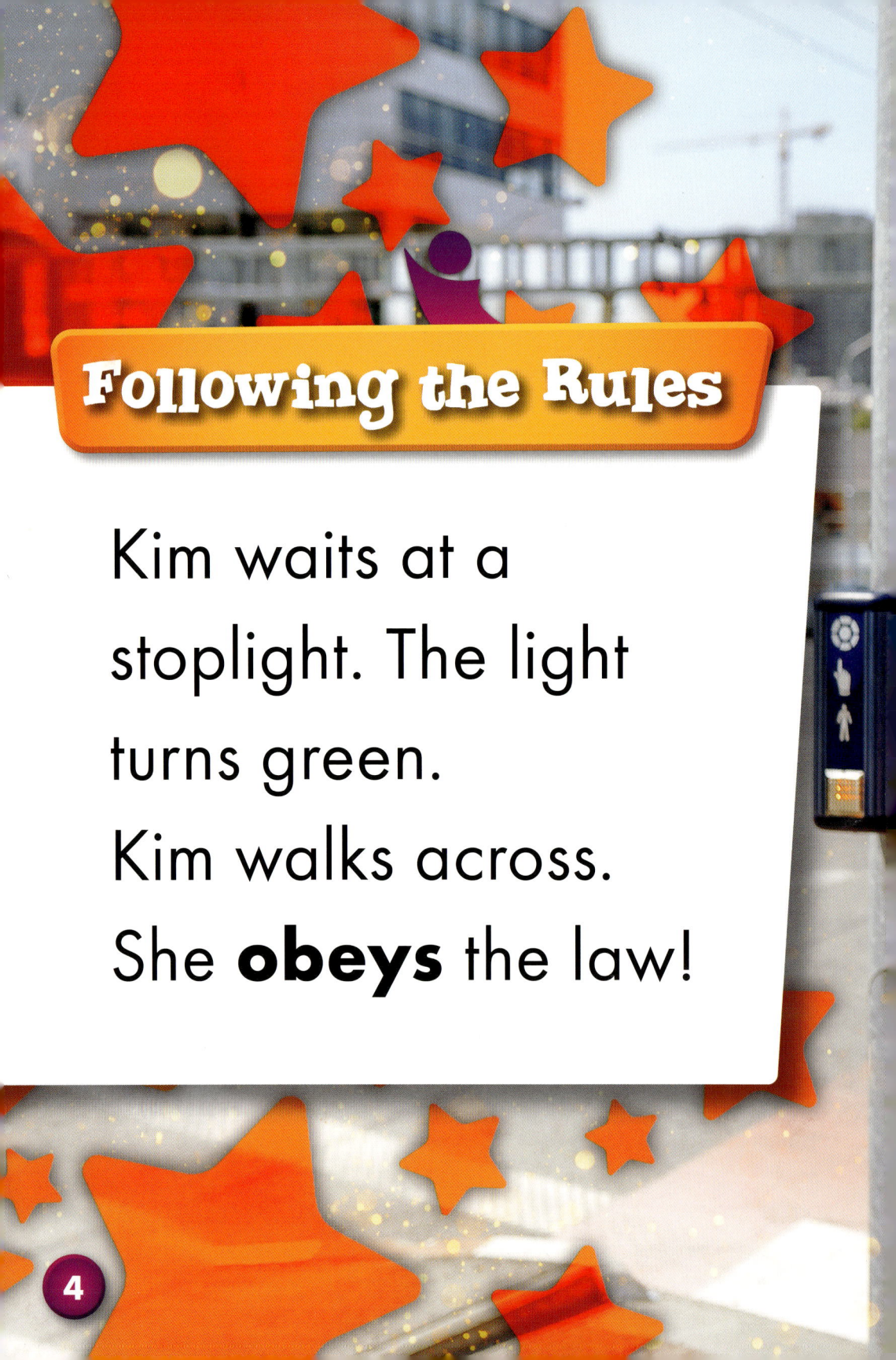

Following the Rules

Kim waits at a stoplight. The light turns green. Kim walks across. She **obeys** the law!

What Are Laws?

Laws are rules that we must follow. They tell us what we can and cannot do.

Cities, states, and countries all have laws. Laws may be different in different places.

Laws are made by the government.

signing a law

Police make sure people follow laws.

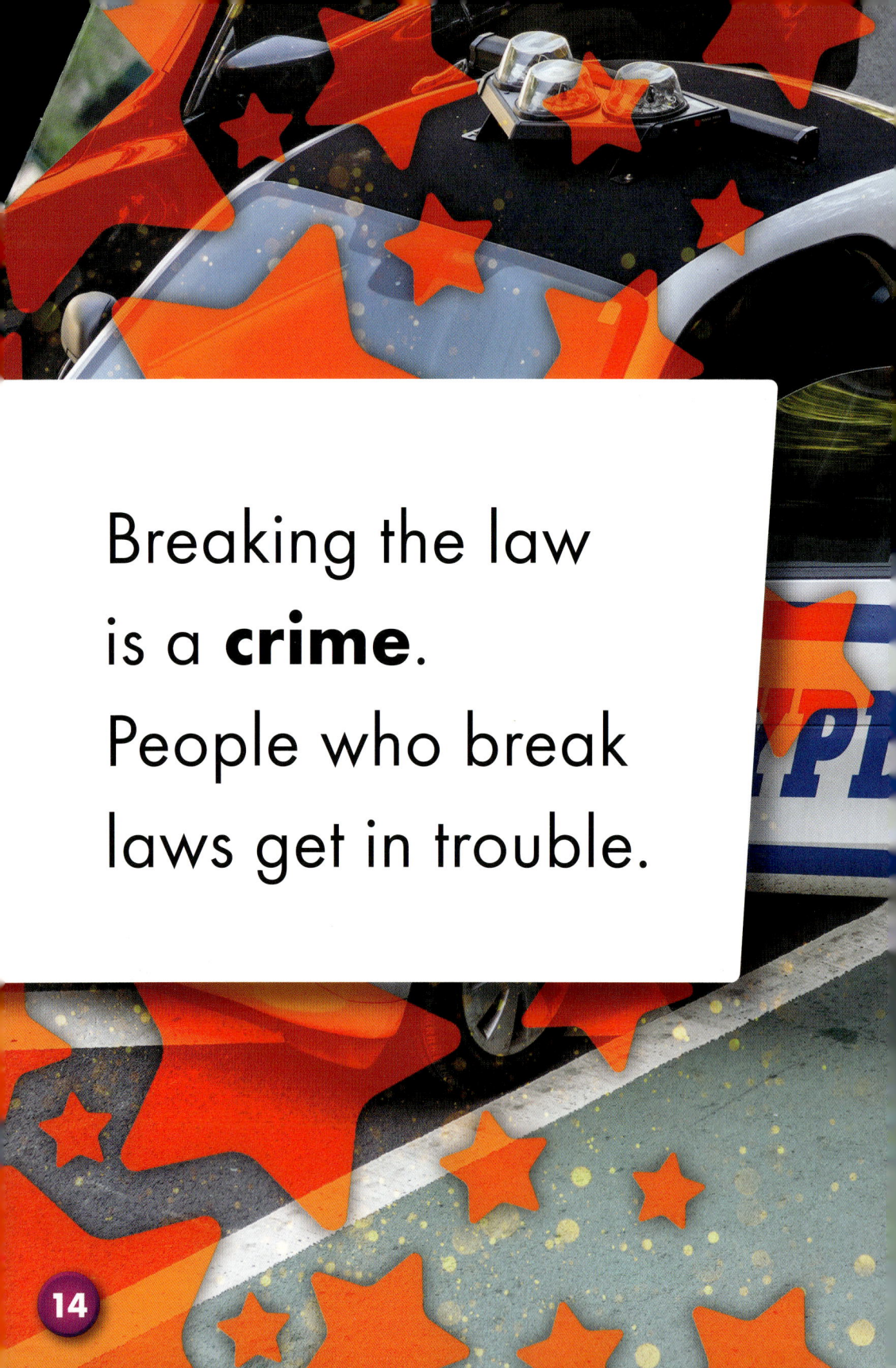

Breaking the law is a **crime**. People who break laws get in trouble.

Why Is Obeying Laws Important?

Laws help keep our **communities** safe.

Laws help protect the **rights** we have as **citizens**.

Laws are meant to make a safe and fair place for everyone to live!

Question

Why do you think obeying the law is important?

Glossary

citizens — people who are members of a certain town, state, or country

obeys — does what is said or written

communities — certain areas and the people who live there

rights — powers people have that should not be taken away

crime — an action that goes against the law

To Learn More

AT THE LIBRARY

Alexander, Vincent. *Obeying Laws.* Minneapolis, Minn.: Jump!, 2019.

Rustad, Martha E. H. *Why Do Communities Need Rules?* North Mankato, Minn.: Capstone, 2020.

Taylor, Charlotte. *Rules and Laws in the United States.* New York, N.Y.: Enslow Publishing, 2021.

ON THE WEB

FACTSURFER

Factsurfer.com gives you a safe, fun way to find more information.

1. Go to www.factsurfer.com.
2. Enter "obeying laws" into the search box and click 🔍.
3. Select your book cover to see a list of related content.

Index

cities, 8
citizens, 18
communities, 16
countries, 8
crime, 14
fair, 20
government, 10
obeys, 4
people, 12
police, 12
protect, 18
question, 21
rights, 18
rules, 6
safe, 16, 20

states, 8
stoplight, 4
trouble, 14
with/without, 19

The images in this book are reproduced through the courtesy of: SDI Productions, front cover; frantic00, pp. 4-5; Svitlana Pimenov, pp. 6-7; coward_lion, pp. 8-9; White House Photo/ Alamy Stock Photo, pp. 10-11; Roman Tiraspolsky, pp. 12-13; rblfmr, pp. 14-15; Jorge Salcedo, pp. 16-17; Stephanie Kenner, pp. 18-19; Michael J P, p. 19 (left); Mike Focus, p. 19 (right); FatCamera, pp. 20-21; Rawpixel.com, p. 22 (citizens); Monkey Business Images, p. 22 (communities); encierro, p. 22 (crime); Sergey Ryzhov, p. 22 (obeys); vesperstock, p. 22 (rights).